YELLOWSTONE NATIONAL PARK

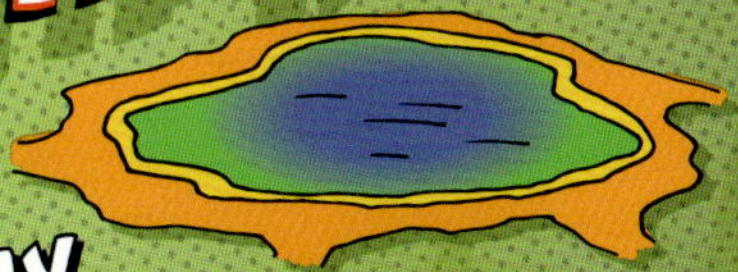

by Diane Bailey

Published by Arcadia Children's Books
A Division of Arcadia Publishing
Charleston, SC
www.arcadiapublishing.com

Copyright © 2022 by Arcadia Children's Books
All rights reserved

Super Cities is a trademark of Arcadia Publishing, Inc.

First published 2022

Manufactured in the United States.

ISBN 978-1-4671-9858-5

Library of Congress Control Number: 2021943255

Notice: The information in this book is true and complete to the best of our knowledge. It is offered without guarantee on the part of the author or Arcadia Publishing. The author and Arcadia Publishing disclaim all liability in connection with the use of this book.

All rights reserved. No part of this book may be reproduced or transmitted in any form whatsoever without prior written permission from the publisher except in the case of brief quotations embodied in critical articles and reviews.

Produced by Shoreline Publishing Group LLC
Santa Barbara, California
Designer: Patty Kelley

Contents

Welcome to Yellowstone! 4
Map It! 6
We're No. 1! 8
Calling It Yellowstone 10
Grand Prismatic Spring 12
History: Ancient History 14
History: First People 16
History: Explorers Arrive 18
History: Let's Make a Park! 20
Yellowstone Today 22
Yellowstone Pioneers 24
Native Americans and
Yellowstone 26
Weather 28
Places to See 30
Getting Around Yellowstone 40
Art from Yellowstone 42
Ansel Adams 44
Museums 46
Meet the Neighbors! 50

Buffalo 52
Welcome Back, Wolves! 54
Other Mammals 56
Birds 58
Frogs, Snakes, and More 60
What People Do in Yellowstone . . 62
Eating in Yellowstone 64
Sweating in Yellowstone 66
Winter in Yellowstone 70
Places to Stay 74
Camping! 76
Campfire Songs and Traditions . . . 78
LOL Yellowstone! 80
Spooky Sites 82
Yellowstone by the Numbers 84
Not Far Away 86
Other Amazing Parks 90

Find Out More 92
Index 94

WELCOME TO Yellowstone!

Anyone want to go to a park? This park does not have any slides or swing sets. There are no large fields for soccer or baseball. Basketball courts? Nope. However, this park does have beautiful views, lots of wildlife, and awesome places to camp. This is not your usual city park but a NATIONAL park. Welcome to Yellowstone, the oldest and most famous national park in the world.

You can find Yellowstone in the western United States. The huge park is mostly in Wyoming, but extends into Idaho and Montana as well. As you'll learn inside this book, the area that

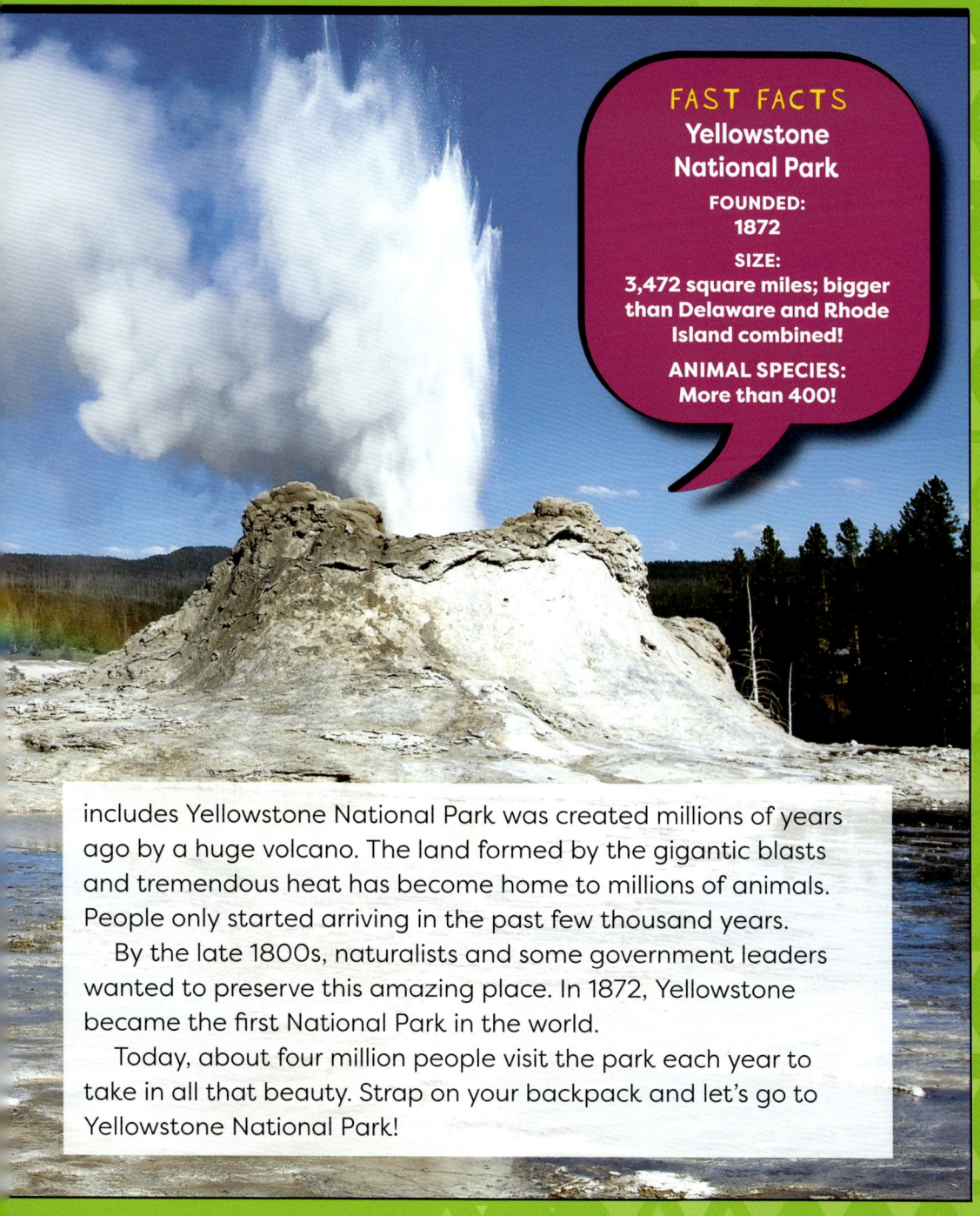

FAST FACTS
Yellowstone National Park
FOUNDED: 1872
SIZE: 3,472 square miles; bigger than Delaware and Rhode Island combined!
ANIMAL SPECIES: More than 400!

includes Yellowstone National Park was created millions of years ago by a huge volcano. The land formed by the gigantic blasts and tremendous heat has become home to millions of animals. People only started arriving in the past few thousand years.

By the late 1800s, naturalists and some government leaders wanted to preserve this amazing place. In 1872, Yellowstone became the first National Park in the world.

Today, about four million people visit the park each year to take in all that beauty. Strap on your backpack and let's go to Yellowstone National Park!

YELLOWSTONE: Map it!

Yellowstone National Park is shaped like a fuzzy-edged square . . . sort of. Most of the park is in the northwest corner of the state of Wyoming. Its rough eastern edge borders the state's Shoshone National Forest. On the north and west, the borders of the park are straighter. In the north, the park stretches into a strip of Montana. On the west, Yellowstone enters the state of Idaho. Directly to the south is Grand Teton National Park, another incredible natural place (see page 88 . . . and who knows, maybe another book in this series!).

Yellowstone has mountains as high as 11,000 feet, but long valleys and huge meadows are more typical landscape features. The Yellowstone River starts at Younts Peak in Wyoming, and flows northwest into Yellowstone Lake before continuing into Montana. Only a few roads have been built to help visitors get around, which protects as much of the park as possible.

Yellowstone National Park

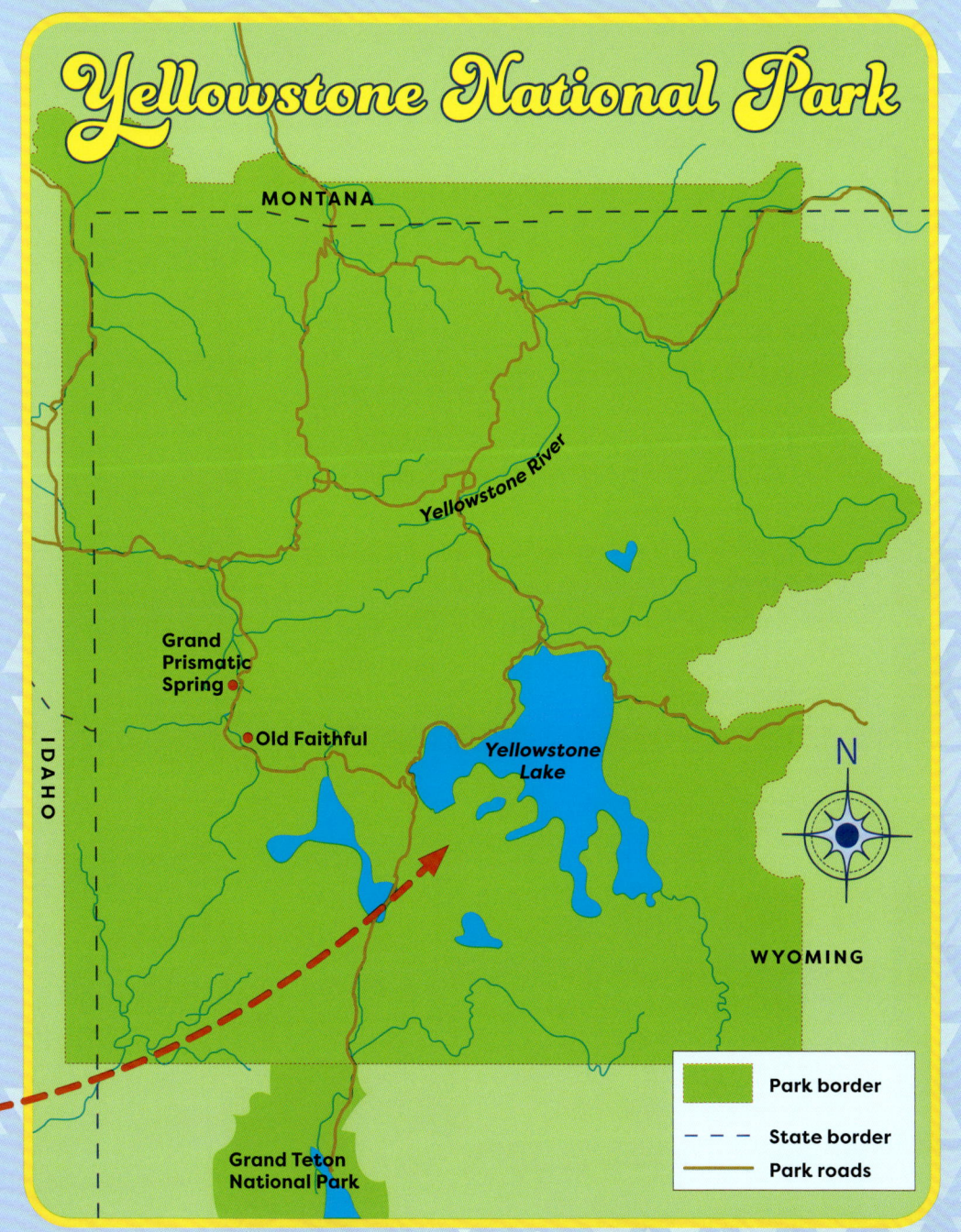

WE'RE NO. 1!

Gushing geysers! Towering mountains! Waterfalls and wildlife! Explorers in the early 1800s knew Yellowstone was something special, but most Americans had no idea where it was or what it looked like.

Over time, word got around about Yellowstone's wonders. In the 1870s, scientists explored the area, bringing back information about its amazing geologic features and stunning landscapes.

Congress was impressed by these reports. They decided it would be a mistake to let Yellowstone be turned into private farms and ranches. Instead, they thought it should be public land, protected so everyone could enjoy it.

In 1864, California had made a state park in a beautiful area called Yosemite. Congress decided to do the same thing with Yellowstone, but on a national level. It would be the country's—make that the world's—first national park.

8 Yellowstone National Park

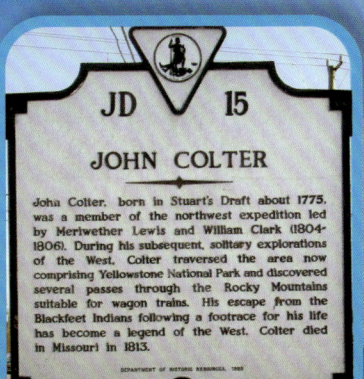

1808: John Colter, an experienced wilderness explorer from the famous Lewis & Clark expedition, is the first known non-indigenous person to visit the Yellowstone region.

1820s through 1860s: Fur trappers and explorers brought back stories of Yellowstone's wonders.

1871: The Hayden expedition, an exploration party to Yellowstone, collected scientific data and visual images of Yellowstone. Congress passed a bill to protect Yellowstone and make it a national park.

March 1, 1872: President Ulysses S. Grant signed Congress's bill into law.

Yellowstone National Park 9

CALLING IT YELLOWSTONE

How did the new national park get its name? Originally, Yellowstone was known as "land of the burning ground" and "land of vapors" to the Crow people. The Flathead people knew it as "smoke from the ground" and the Kiowa people called it "the place of hot water."

The name actually comes from the main river that flows through the park. The Hidatsa, a Sioux tribe, named it Yellow Rock River, after the sandstone that lines the waterway. As the name passed through other languages, it became Yellowstone. When it became a national park, its founders chose that most recent name.

But whatever you call Yellowstone . . . you have to call it beautiful and amazing—and that's not blowing smoke!

A painting of a chief of the Hidatsa.

Steam rises from one of Yellowstone's many geysers.

10 Yellowstone National Park

FAST FACT In Hidatsa, the words "Mi tsi a-da-zi" mean "Yellow Rock River."

The Yellowstone River as it flows through the park.

Yellowstone National Park

GRAND PRISMATIC SPRING

How grand is Grand? The Grand Prismatic Spring is about 370 feet across (bigger than a football field) and more than 120 feet deep (about 12 stories). That makes it the largest hot spring in the United States.

In living color: All those bright colors come from different species of microbes that live in the water. The colors change according to the season. There is usually more green in the winter, and more orange in the summer.

12 Yellowstone National Park

Get your camera out! The Grand Prismatic Spring is one of the most photographed places in Yellowstone. That's no surprise—this giant hot spring is like a living prism! It is deep blue in the middle, and then spreads out into all the colors of the rainbow. You can view the lake from ground level, or hike just over a mile up the Grand Prismatic Overlook Trail to get a spectacular view from 200 feet up.

Where does it come from? Water continuously flows into the spring from a crack in the bottom. It gushes out about 560 gallons a minute!

Feel the heat: The center of the spring is the hottest, reaching temperatures of about 188 degrees F.

Yellowstone National Park

HISTORY: Ancient History

It took millions of years and three supervolcanoes to form the awesome landscape of Yellowstone . . . and it's not done yet!

150 million years ago: Hotspots of magma, or melted rock, began forming under the area that is now Yellowstone. Over the years, they drifted closer to the surface. Look out—she's gonna blow!

Magma-nificent! When magma spews out from deep within the earth, it's like a geologic game of Jenga gone wrong. Magma supports the rock and earth on top of it. When it spurts up, the earth collapses down. That creates a huge bowl in the ground called a caldera.

2.1 million years ago: A supervolcano erupted, forming the Island Park Caldera, which includes parts of Yellowstone. Scientists believe it was one of the largest volcanic eruptions in the history of the planet.

1.3 million years ago: A smaller eruption formed another caldera on the western side of the Island Park caldera. It's not technically part of Yellowstone National Park, but it was part of the series of eruptions that led to...

640,000 years ago: The main Yellowstone Caldera formed when a supervolcano erupted.

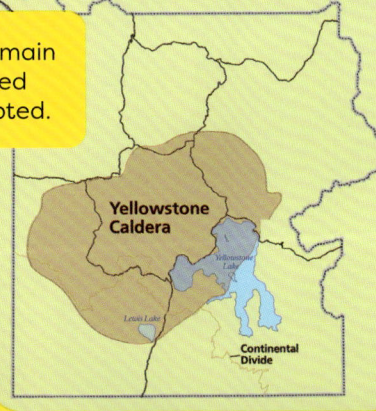

What's next? No one knows for sure. The Yellowstone supervolcano will erupt again, sometime, but scientists don't think it will be in the next few hundred years.

Tuff Stuff: Many of the mountains and cliffs in Yellowstone are made of tuff, a lightweight rock that forms when ash from volcanos hardens.

Yellowstone National Park 15

HISTORY: First People

People have been living in Yellowstone for at least 10,000 years. More than two dozen Native American peoples—including the Shoshone, Bannock, Nez Perce, Kiowa (pictured from 1890s), Crow, Flathead (Salish), Blackfeet, and Lakota Sioux—can trace some of their ancestors back to Yellowstone.

Remains of a camp on the shores of **Yellowstone Lake** date back more than 9,000 years. There are also artifacts on islands in the lake, suggesting early people used boats or rafts.

Stones found on **Obsidian Cliff** were an important resource for Yellowstone's early residents. Obsidian is a stone formed from hardened lava, and shards of it can be sharper than a razor blade. That made it valuable for making tools such as knives and spear points.

The Tukudika, or Mountain Shoshone (sometimes called "sheepeaters") are most likely the only indigenous people who lived in Yellowstone year-round, probably in the early 1800s. They hunted bighorn sheep, which they ate during the harsh winters when little food was available. They also made bows from the horns of the sheep.

Through the mid 1800s, other peoples visited Yellowstone in the warmer seasons. Many traveled through on bison hunts across the Western Plains.

A Shoshone village in Wyoming from 1870.

Mythbusters: Early white visitors spread a rumor that indigenous people feared Yellowstone's steaming geysers, believing they were evil forces. In fact, indigenous people honored the earth and visited these sites as part of spiritual ceremonies.

Yellowstone National Park 17

HISTORY: Explorers Arrive

Native Americans had lived in and visited Yellowstone for centuries, but European Americans eventually arrived in the area. The first known white explorer to visit Yellowstone was John Colter, a fur trapper who came in the winter of 1807-08.

With all its wildlife, Yellowstone was a great place for fur trappers like Osborne Russell, Daniel Potts, and Jim Bridger. They all explored the area in the 1820s and 1830s. When they tried to talk about rainbow-colored pools and steam hissing out of mountains, people didn't believe them!

Jim Bridger

Gold prospectors arrived in the 1860s. There had been gold strikes nearby in Montana and Wyoming, and Yellowstone seemed like a good bet. No one ever discovered gold in Yellowstone itself, though (or if they did, they kept it a secret!).

Yellowstone National Park

Enough stories about Yellowstone's beauty had been passed around that a formal expedition to explore Yellowstone arrived in 1869. Another followed in 1870. Then, in 1871, Ferdinand Hayden, a geologist with the U.S. government, led the first scientific expedition to Yellowstone. His 32-member team included experts to study rocks, minerals, plants, animals, insects, and more.

A photographer, William Henry Jackson, and a landscape painter, Thomas Moran, also joined the Hayden expedition. They produced amazing pictures that helped convince Congress to officially protect Yellowstone and make it a national park.

Cascade Creek by Thomas Moran

Lower Falls of the Yellowstone by William Henry Jackson

Yellowstone National Park

HISTORY: Let's Make a Park!

Even after it became official (see page 8), Yellowstone was a long way from becoming the tourist hotspot it is now. The park was still rugged wilderness. Visitors had to be fearless adventurers and enthusiastic campers. But soon there were roads and rangers to help make Yellowstone easier to get around in—and a lot more popular!

This photo from 1887 shows some of the early buildings.

1871: Even before Yellowstone was a national park, it already had its first hotel. The McCartney Hotel was just a log cabin, but guests were welcome—as long as they brought their own blankets and didn't mind sleeping on the floor.

1882: Ten years after opening, Yellowstone attracted about 1,000 visitors a year.

1883: Rail lines reached Yellowstone, making it easier for travelers to reach the park. The park also welcomed its first tourists to explore on bicycles! Unfortunately, more visitors meant more problems. Poachers (people who kill animals illegally) and squatters (people who lived there illegally) invaded the park.

1886: Congress got fed up with park officials who weren't taking good care of Yellowstone and put the U.S. Army in charge.

1903: President Theodore Roosevelt visited and dedicated the "Roosevelt Arch" at the park's north entrance.

1904: Construction was finished on the Old Faithful Inn.

1915: The first cars arrived in Yellowstone—before that, people came mostly in stagecoaches! None of the park's roads were paved, however, so the cars got stuck in the mud a lot.

Yellowstone National Park

YELLOWSTONE TODAY

Yellowstone celebrates its 150th anniversary as a national park in 2022. At first, only a few thousand people per year visited—the park was hard to travel *to* and even harder to travel *in*. Today? About four million visitors come each year.

The National Park Service has been in charge of the park since 1918. More than 750 rangers and scientific experts help protect the park and make sure visitors are safe. More join in the summer when crowds are at their biggest.

The middle of summer is prime time for Yellowstone: it's comfortable to be outside, the vegetation is lush, and wildlife are active. But winter can be pretty amazing, too—if you're willing to arrive by snowmobile, that is.

Yellowstone has an enormous amount of stuff to see and do inside its boundaries. Visitors can gaze at geysers spurting out from deep in the earth, ooh and aah over stunning waterfalls, hike backcountry trails, climb mountains, and see all kinds of wildlife. Yellowstone's nickname is "Wonderland"—and it's no *wonder* where that came from!

Yellowstone Pioneers

Yellowstone wouldn't be what it is today without a lot of people who helped shape the park. Here are a few who made a difference during Yellowstone's early years:

John Colter (1774-1813)
Mountain man John Colter was part of the famous Lewis & Clark expedition that explored the American West beginning in 1803. In 1807 he was on another expedition to the Rocky Mountains when he ended up in Yellowstone—the first non-indigenous man known to set foot there.

Ferdinand Hayden (1829-1887)
As a geologist (someone who studies the earth) for the U.S. government, Ferdinand Hayden organized an 1871 expedition to study Yellowstone—the first that had scientific research as its main goal. Today, you'll see his name all over places in Yellowstone.

Philetus Norris (1821-1885)

Another name you'll see is Philetus Norris, the second superintendent of Yellowstone and the first to get paid for the job. He worked to build more roads and trails in the park to make it easier to get around. He also worried that Yellowstone would be ruined by hunters and trappers, and pushed for rules that would protect the land and animals that lived there.

Harry Yount (1839-1924)

Harry Yount became Yellowstone's "gamekeeper" in 1880. Basically, he was the very first park ranger. Although some hunting was legal inside Yellowstone until 1883, Yount was in charge of stopping illegal hunters from killing too many animals in the park. Protecting animals and ecosystems is still one of the main jobs of the National Park Service.

Native American Peoples and Yellowstone

Native American peoples have thought of Yellowstone as a sacred, spiritual place for centuries. Different cultures performed ceremonies around geysers and used hot springs as places for healing. Some young men traveled there on vision quests to communicate with spirits. Once Yellowstone became a national park, however, many native peoples were pushed out onto reservations or prevented from reaching their traditional sacred or hunting sites. Today, many people are working to revive Native American history in Yellowstone.

Bountiful Bison These animals were once endangered, but now there are actually too many in Yellowstone. To keep the numbers under control, park managers are working with tribes like the Assiniboine and Sioux, who traditionally hunted bison, to transfer animals to their reservation in Montana.

A Kiowa Story A Kiowa legend says that, long ago, a spirit brought the Kiowa people to the barren land of Yellowstone and dared a young man to jump into the boiling pool now called Dragon's Mouth. He did, and the landscape became green and beautiful. The spirit then gave the Kiowa the land as their home.

DRAGON'S MOUTH SPRING
An unknown park visitor named this feature around 1912, perhaps due to the water that frequently surged from the cave like the lashing of a dragon's tongue. Until 1994, this dramatic wave-like action often splashed water as far as the boardwalk. The rumbling sounds are caused by steam and other gasses exploding through the water, causing it to crash against the walls of the hidden caverns.

Powwows For a look into Native American culture, visit the Wind River Reservation to the southeast of Yellowstone. It's home to the Northern Arapaho and Eastern Shoshone people. Throughout the summer, visitors can attend powwows that celebrate Arapaho and Shoshone life.

Naming Traditions Today, only a handful of places in Yellowstone are named after Native Americans—places like Shoshone Lake and Wahhi Falls. Instead, landmarks honor the white explorers who came later. Some Native American groups are working to change the names of some Yellowstone landmarks to remember the people who were there first. One proposal will change Mount Doane to First Peoples Mountain.

Yellowstone park rangers meet often with Native American groups to both teach and learn.

Yellowstone Weather All Four Seasons!

Yellowstone sits *waayyyy* above sea level—the average elevation is more than 8,000 feet. In the summer, the weather is usually pretty pleasant. In the winter—bundle up! Here's a look at what to expect (all temperatures are in degrees F.):

Even in summer, Yellowstone rarely gets hot. Daytime highs are usually between 70 and 80 degrees, and nights can get chilly enough for a sweater. Spring and fall daytime temperatures range from 30 to 60 degrees, while winter hovers between zero and 20 degrees.

That's extreme! The record high temperature in Yellowstone was set in 2002, at 99 degrees. The record low came in 1993: -66 degrees.

28 Yellowstone National Park

Wet or Dry? Depends on where you are in the park. The north is pretty dry, receiving only about 10 inches of rain per year. The southwest corner is much drippier, with about 80 inches. (For comparison, the national average is around 30 inches.)

Snow Days Yellowstone has a lot of them. The average annual snowfall is about 12 feet. At the higher elevations, it can be over 20 feet! It's not uncommon to see snow still on the ground in June. But it doesn't snow in July, right? Well, not usually.

Wildfires They can be scary, but they're an important part of the Yellowstone ecosystem. Many plants have adapted to fire and actually need it to grow properly. Park rangers allow fires to burn naturally when possible, while still protecting people and buildings.

Yellowstone National Park

FAST FACT
The plume of water from Old Faithful can reach more than 100 feet high, and it's hot—more than 200 degrees F.

OLD FAITHFUL GEYSER

Yellowstone National Park

Things to see in Yellowstone

Old Faithful

Old Faithful isn't the biggest geyser in Yellowstone, but it's definitely the most reliable. It erupts approximately 20 times a day, for about two to three minutes each time. A short eruption leaves some hot water in the geyser's "tank" under the earth, meaning the next eruption comes about an hour later. If it's a longer eruption, it takes roughly an hour and a half for the water to build up again.

On Time: The geyser is so "faithful" to its schedule because it's not connected to other thermal features in the park. That means the same amount of water builds up between each eruption.

Keep it Clean: Early visitors to Yellowstone used Old Faithful to do their laundry. They put their dirty clothes in the geyser when it was calm, and then waited for it to spit them back out, thoroughly washed!

What's the Difference?
Geysers and hot springs both come from water heated underground by the earth. Hot water turns to steam, which builds up pressure. The boiling water and steam escape out the surface. With hot springs, the water is able to spread out, forming a pool. Geysers have small exit tubes, so the water spurts out powerfully.

More Geysers

Yellowstone has almost 500 geysers throughout the park. That's about half the number in the entire world! There are so many that not all of them even have names. Check out some of these other cool (hot, actually!) geysers in Yellowstone:

Just up the road from Old Faithful is the world's tallest active geyser. Water from **Steamboat Geyser** can shoot up to 300 feet in the air. It's not nearly as predictable as "OF," though. There are usually at least several days between eruptions, and sometimes several years!

Morning Glory Pool is a small, but deep, pool with amazing colors. It used to be mostly a deep blue, but the water has cooled over the years, so now there is more green and yellow.

Yellowstone National Park

You're more likely to spot **Grand Geyser**, the park's tallest geyser that is somewhat predictable. Ten-minute-long eruptions shoot water about 200 feet in the air, and you can count on it getting active every 8 to 15 hours.

Enjoy the view standing slightly above **Riverside Geyser**, which makes a fountain of water into the nearby Firehole River.

Get Muddy: Water bubbles slowly come to the surface at mudpots. Sulfur in the mud makes them smelly (think rotten eggs), but the chemicals also create beautiful colors. Artist Paint Pot, Fountain Paint Pot, and Mud Volcano are some of the park's most impressive mudpots.

Yellowstone National Park 33

Water World

Yellowstone is known as "Wonderland," but it could be called "Waterland." Here's a look at the park's wetter attractions:

Yellowstone Lake It might look fun, but don't jump in for a swim. The average water temperature is barely over 40 degrees F! Instead, visitors can take boats on the lake or walk on the 100-plus miles of coast. You might have to share the shore with moose and bears, so look out!

Yellowstone River
Almost 700 miles long, the Yellowstone River is the longest river in the country with no dams on it, making it a great place to look for wildlife. You'll find lots of places to pull off the road and take a short hike or just enjoy the view.

There are almost 300 waterfalls in Yellowstone. Some are only reachable by hiking, but several of the most popular ones are right on the road:

Yellowstone Falls The most famous waterfalls in the park come in two parts: Upper and Lower. The Lower Falls (right) are the tallest in the park at 308 feet high—twice as high as Niagara Falls! The Upper Falls aren't as tall, but they're still amazing to see.

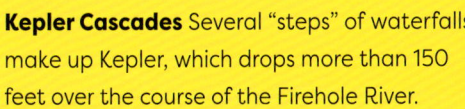

Tower Fall Tall rock cliffs on either side emphasize the 132-foot height of this waterfall. It certainly makes a splash when it hits the Yellowstone River below.

Kepler Cascades Several "steps" of waterfalls make up Kepler, which drops more than 150 feet over the course of the Firehole River.

Yellowstone National Park

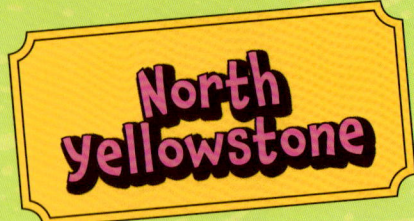
North Yellowstone

The north part of Yellowstone deserves a day to itself. Put these highlights on your to-do list:

Obsidian Cliff This black cliff is made from obsidian, a hard, smooth, glass-like substance made when lava cools quickly. Native Americans from nearby used to travel here to collect obsidian to make tools.

Perfectly Preserved If you're up for a fairly challenging hike, check out the Fossil Forest near the Tower-Roosevelt area. Volcanic eruptions 50 million years ago buried the area in lava and ash, "freezing" plants and animals into petrified specimens.

Saddle Up Do it like the old timers did! At Roosevelt Corral (named for President Theodore Roosevelt), you can take a guided tour of the area from horseback.

Yellowstone National Park

Mammoth Hot Springs

Travertine terraces? What are those? Basically, they're stone stairs. *Travertine* is a type of limestone, and *terraces* is a fancy word for "steps." At **Mammoth Hot Springs** (right), water bubbles up and dissolves chemicals in the limestone to form complex layers of colored terraces.

Liberty Cap: Most of the terraces are relatively flat, but at Liberty Cap, water rose from the earth in the same place for a long time, forming this 37-foot tall rock. The name comes from a floppy hat popular during the French Revolution in the late 1700s.

Canary Spring: This one's named for its bright yellow color that reminded explorers of a canary's feathers.

Yellowstone National Park 37

Down Below

THE GRAND CANYON OF THE YELLOWSTONE

The canyon varies from 800 to 1200 feet in depth and from 1500 to 4000 feet in width. Its length is about 24 miles. The upper 2½ miles is the most colorful section. Hot spring activity has continued through the ages altering the lava rock to produce lovely colors which are largely due to varied iron compounds. Have you noticed that steam vents and geysers are still at work on the canyon walls?

It's taken about 150,000 years to make the **Grand Canyon of the Yellowstone**. The Lower Falls of the Yellowstone River have dumped a lot of water in that time, carving a path that's more than 20 miles long, 1,000 feet deep, and up to 4,000 feet wide!

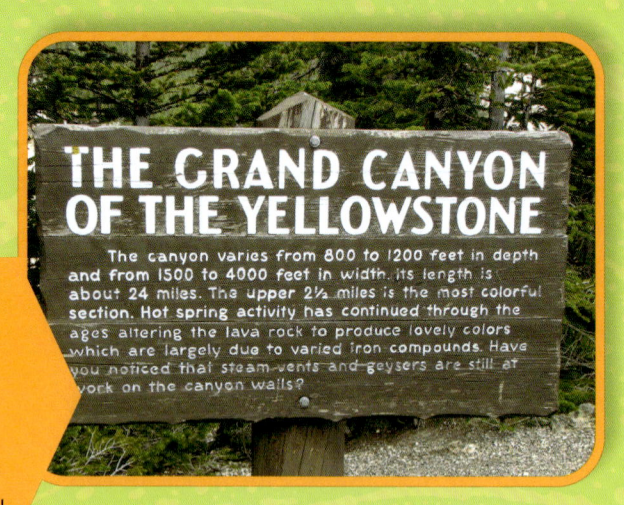

Feeling a little rusty: The red color of the canyon walls comes from iron in the rocks. When the iron comes into contact with oxygen, it goes through a chemical reaction that turns it into rust.

Bring the binoculars: You might spot an osprey! They mate here in spring, and chicks are born in early summer. The babies are helpless, so their parents fish in the canyon's river and bring them food.

Life in the Valleys

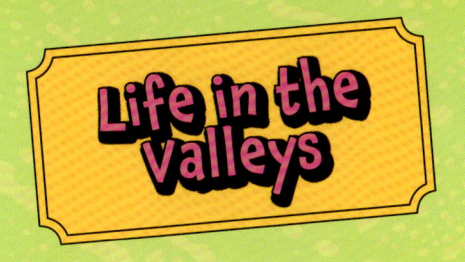

Large meadows in eastern and central Yellowstone are great for wildlife viewing. The **Hayden** and **Lamar Valleys** have huge herds of grazing animals and packs of predators looking for dinner! Hayden is bigger, but it's a little more crowded. Lamar is more out of the way. You can't go wrong with either one, though. Wildlife wanders freely, so no matter where you go, you're sure to see some creatures.

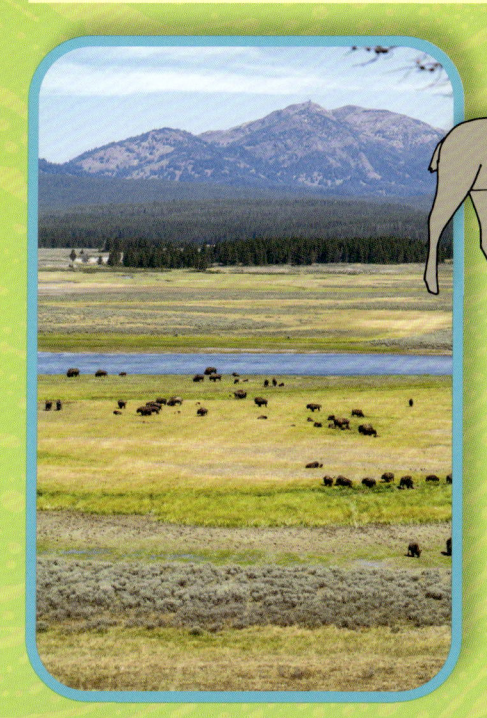

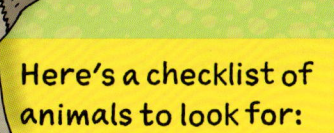

Here's a checklist of animals to look for:

- Bison
- Elk
- Pronghorn sheep
- Moose
- Grizzly bears
- Wolves
- Coyotes
- Deer
- Eagles
- Ospreys

Yellowstone National Park

GETTING AROUND YELLOWSTONE

There's plenty of Yellowstone that you can see out the car window. These scenic routes will help make the most of your drive time:

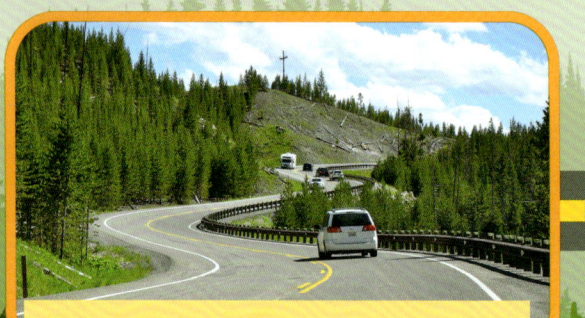

The **Grand Loop** is a 142-mile circle around the middle of Yellowstone. It's split into two loops that make a figure eight, so just one of them is a good amount for a single day. The Upper Loop goes past Mammoth Hot Springs, the Tower-Roosevelt area, and Lamar Valley. The Lower Loop includes Old Faithful, the Hayden Valley, the Firehole area, and Yellowstone Lake. Norris Geyser Basin and the Canyon district are in the middle and can be reached from either loop.

On the Upper Loop, take a detour onto **Blacktail Plateau Drive**. This is a six-mile, one-way side trip off the main road heading east from Mammoth. You'll have to drive slowly on this dirt road, but that makes it easier to see wildlife!

The gorgeous 27-mile drive from **East Entrance Road** passes through the mountains before settling down into the valley and Yellowstone Lake.

Old-Time Buses
Newly restored, some of the park's long yellow tour buses are back in action. Some date back to the 1930s!

The park is going green—and driverless! An experimental no-driver electric tram took riders on short routes through Canyon Village. The trams are known as "TEDDY."

Yellowstone National Park

Art from Yellowstone

Artists love the amazing scenery at Yellowstone—and it changes every day!

Grafton Tyler Brown was one of the first African American artists to paint images from Yellowstone. His paintings from the 1880s were popular with tourists.

No experience necessary! Amateur artists can stop in at the **Yellowstone Art & Photography Center** in Old Faithful Village, where artists-in-residence teach free classes in drawing and painting Yellowstone landmarks.

Check out more at the **Yellowstone Art Museum** in Billings, Montana, and the **Whitney Western Art Museum** (part of the Buffalo Bill Center of the West) in Cody, Wyoming.

42 Yellowstone National Park

The first detailed images of Yellowstone were made during the 1871 Hayden expedition. **William Henry Jackson** was the first person to photograph Yellowstone. His pictures provided proof of Yellowstone's amazing features.

Landscape painter **Thomas Moran** was also part of the Hayden expedition. He brought the colors of Yellowstone alive. Congress bought one of his paintings, "The Grand Canyon of the Yellowstone," for $10,000. It's huge—12 feet by 7 feet! It hangs in the Smithsonian American Art Museum in Washington, D.C.

Today, artists can get a permit to paint in the park. This process is called *plein air*, which is French for "outdoors." There's even a place just for artists—**Artist Point** has a fabulous view of the Lower Falls.

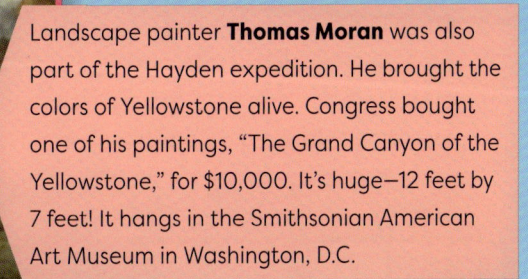

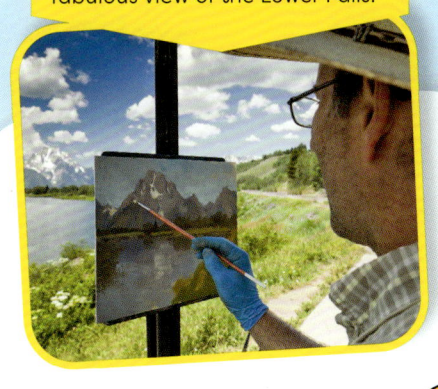

Photographer **Frank Haynes** set up Yellowstone's first photo shop in 1884, near Mammoth. He made postcards of his photos to sell as souvenirs. He also sold cameras and film so tourists could take their own shots.

Yellowstone National Park

Ansel Adams

Ansel Adams (1902-1984) was born in San Francisco and was a teenager when he first started taking photographs. Later he became a technical expert, writing books and teaching classes. His style of photography emphasized crisp lines and sharp contrast between black and white tones in the images. He especially loved taking pictures of nature and the outdoors. In the 1940s, the National Park Service hired him to take photos of several national parks, including Yellowstone.

Adams liked to envision what he thought a photo should look like. Then he used different developing techniques to make his vision come alive.

All of Adams' Yellowstone photos were in black and white, which he preferred over color. None of them included people.

Yellowstone isn't the only national park Adams photographed. He also took photos of the Grand Canyon, Glacier National Park, and Yosemite National Park, among others.

World War II cut short Adams' job with the Park Service. He had only a few days to photograph Yellowstone, but he managed to get 27 photos for the park service (and nine for himself!).

Adams took several photos of Old Faithful erupting. He labeled them "taken at dawn or dusk." He couldn't remember which!

Yellowstone National Park

Yellowstone Museums

Take a break inside for a few hours! Yellowstone has several museums where you can learn more about its history and natural features.

Albright Visitor Center When the army was in charge of the park in the early 1900s, soldiers lived in this building, which was part of Fort Yellowstone, first built in 1891 and later given to the National Park Service. Now, there's lots of information on the history of people and animals in the park, and cool exhibits like life-size models of bison, bighorn sheep, and wolves.

Museum of the National Park Ranger Learn about the history of the National Park Service and the jobs of park rangers. Got questions? Many of the volunteers at the museum are retired rangers, so they should have answers!

Yellowstone National Park

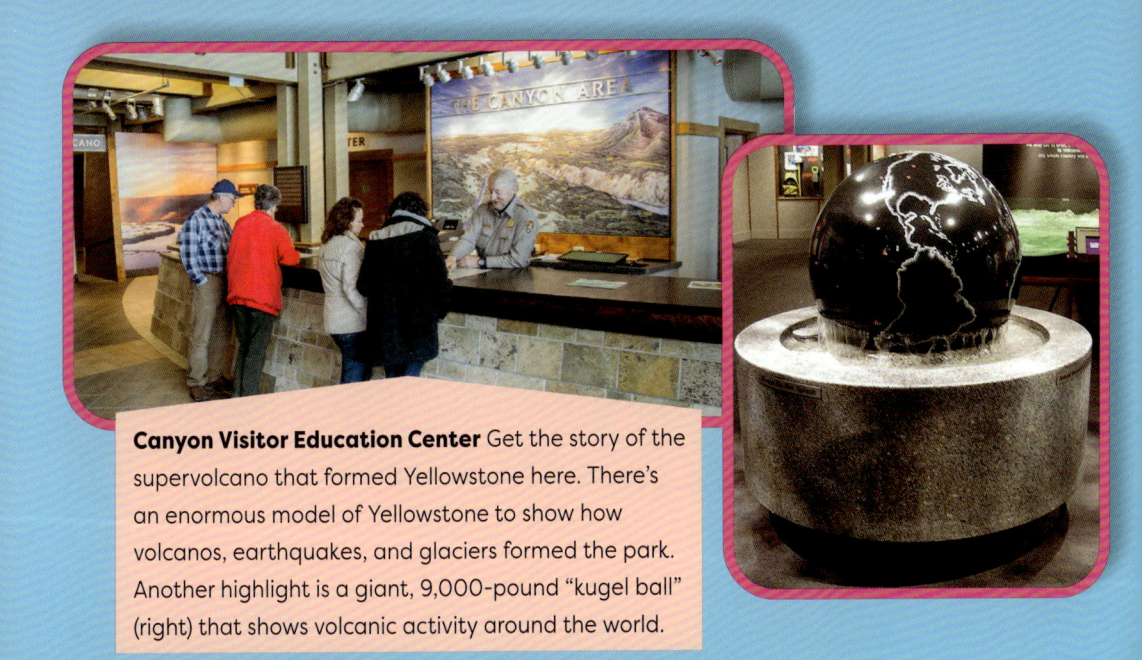

Canyon Visitor Education Center Get the story of the supervolcano that formed Yellowstone here. There's an enormous model of Yellowstone to show how volcanos, earthquakes, and glaciers formed the park. Another highlight is a giant, 9,000-pound "kugel ball" (right) that shows volcanic activity around the world.

Norris Geyser Basin Museum Norris was one of several small museums that park managers opened for visitors to learn about the park when they were not on guided tours. Think of Norris as "Geology Central"—the place to learn about geysers and other thermal features in the park.

Yellowstone National Park

Amazing Women of Yellowstone

The people who first explored Yellowstone were men, but women soon began to play a part in making sure that visitors were kept safe and that the park and its animals thrived. Today, about a third of all National Park Rangers are women. In 2019, Sarah Davis (left) was named Yellowstone's chief resource and visitor protection officer—the head ranger. She was the first woman to get that important job; she served until 2021.

Former chief ranger Sarah Davis

In 1925, after working part-time for four years, Marguerite Lindsley was named the first female permanent Park Ranger. She knew her stuff; she had lived in the park as a child when her father worked there!

48 Yellowstone National Park

In the 1920s and early 1930s, plant expert Herma Baggley served as a ranger as well as the park's first female naturalist. She wrote books about Yellowstone's plant life that are still used today.

Yellowstone National Park 49

Meet the Neighbors!

Wildlife is one big reason people visit Yellowstone. You can see thousands of animals in their native habitats—with no fences!

Animals in the park are protected by law from hunters. These laws have helped protect endangered populations that live in the park, such as the Canada lynx and black-footed ferret.

Yellowstone has hundreds of animal species.
Birds: 300
Mammals: 67
Fish: 16
Reptiles: 6
Amphibians: 5

Mountain bluebird

50 Yellowstone National Park

Yellowstone has such a variety of animals because it has so many different habitats, including grasslands, mountains, forests, rivers, and lakes.

Many animals don't stay within the park's boundaries. They use the entire Greater Yellowstone ecosystem, which is roughly ten times the size of the park itself.

Keep Your Distance! Park rules prohibit coming within 100 yards (that's a whole football field!) of bears or wolves, and 25 yards for other wildlife.

Phabulous Photos

Try these tips for getting good photos with a smartphone camera:
▶ **Zoom.** Use your camera lens—not your feet!—to get closer.
▶ **Be Quiet.** Be as still and quiet as possible so you don't scare animals. Make sure your phone is on silent mode, too—they can hear that little "click."
▶ **Be Patient.** Don't try to coax animals into doing something. Wait until they're ready and you'll end up with better pictures.
▶ **Overdo It**. Use "burst" mode to get several shots in just a few seconds. You can go back later and pick out the best ones.

Yellowstone National Park

Bison

Tens of millions of bison used to live in North America. Native Americans depended on the animals for food and fur. Then white hunters arrived and killed so many bison in the 1800s that the animals almost went extinct. In 1902, Yellowstone park managers started a conservation and breeding program to bring back bison. It worked. Now, about 4,600 bison live in the park. That's the largest population anywhere in the United States!

FAST FACT
Bison vs buffalo? The scientific name for these animals is *Bison bison*. They are also called buffalo, but are not really buffaloes. Animals by that name live in Africa.

Bison are the largest land animals in the United States. Males weigh about 2,000 pounds, and females about 1,100 pounds.

Congress passed the National Bison Legacy Act in 2016, officially making bison the country's "national mammal."

Not just cars clog the roads in Yellowstone. It's pretty common to get stuck in a "bison jam" as the animals wander (slowly!) from one grazing area to another.

Bison might look slow, but they're very athletic. They can run up to 35 miles per hour, and jump as high as five feet!

Bison often graze in the same area several times. That makes the grass grow back faster, which helps makes sure that there's always grass for the bison to eat.

Yellowstone National Park

Welcome Back Wolves

Wolves roamed through Yellowstone for thousands of years, but hunters had mostly killed them off by the 1920s. It stayed that way for several decades. Then, in 1995, Yellowstone park managers led a conservation program to re-introduce wolves to this natural habitat. Now there are about 100 wolves in the park—the right number for that amount of land.

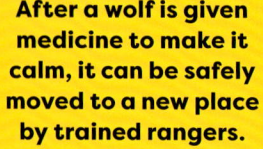

After a wolf is given medicine to make it calm, it can be safely moved to a new place by trained rangers.

Why do wolves matter?

When a wolf kills a deer or elk, they don't just feed themselves. Lots of other animals get some, too. If bears get a sniff, they often chase away the wolves and take over. Coyotes lurk until the wolves (and bears) are finished eating and then take their turn. Eagles, ravens, and other birds pick over what's left.

When the wolves were gone, parts of the ecosystem collapsed. But once they came back, the balance was restored. Wolves kept the elk population stable, which helped restore water plants that elk were eating. This helped beavers have space to build more dams, which helped riverbanks. Birds enjoyed the trees that grew instead of being eaten by elk. The shade from the trees helped make ponds and streams better for fish. And all because wolves came back at the top of the food chain.

FAST FACT
Apex predators: Wolves are at the top of the food chain. The only predators for healthy, adult wolves are other wolves (and people).

Yellowstone National Park

Other Mammals

Yellowstone has the most mammals of anywhere in the Lower 48 (every state except Alaska and Hawaii). Here's a look at some of them:

Wolverines and lynx are two of the rarest animals in the park. The chance of seeing one of these is low, but automatic park cameras in the woods occasionally capture an image of them.

Black bear

Lynx

About 500 black bears and 150 grizzly bears live in Yellowstone. Black bears usually stick to the woods, while grizzlies can be spotted in meadows.

Grizzly bear

Hoofed animals like mule deer and elk are common throughout the park. There are also some pronghorn. Habitat loss has hurt the populations of moose, unfortunately, and only about 200 live in the park. Bighorn sheep are also rare, and harder to spot because of their remote habitat in the mountains.

Moose

Elk

Yellowstone's rivers are good places to observe beavers and river otters.

Otter

Squirrel

Small mammals thrive in Yellowstone. Look for squirrels, chipmunks, raccoons, and weasels. You might catch a glimpse of the Northern Flying Squirrel in the trees at night.

It's a Sign

The pika is a small animal similar to a rabbit. Pikas are common in Yellowstone, but they're starting to move out of the park's lower elevations. Biologists think that's because climate change is making those areas too warm. Pikas are considered an "indicator species." That means their behavior often shows how an environment is changing.

Birds

About 150 species of birds nest and mate in the park, and lots more pass through when they're migrating (moving from one area to another for different seasons).

Large raptors—also called birds of prey—include owls, hawks, eagles, ospreys, and falcons.

Bald eagle

Owlets

Red-tailed hawk

Yellowstone National Park

Trumpeter swan

FAST FACT
Download a list of birds that live in Yellowstone from the internet, and see how many you can spot!

Near water, look for trumpeter swans, Canada geese, pelicans, loons, herons, egrets, and ducks.

Dusky grouse

Most of Yellowstone's birds are small. Some live in trees, while others like openings in cliffs or nests on the ground. There are woodpeckers, chickadees, nuthatches, crows, ravens, blue jays, hummingbirds, and more.

Swing by the **Fishing Bridge Visitor Center**, where Yellowstone's birds are on display. There are taxidermy (stuffed) specimens of American white pelicans, trumpeter swans, and many smaller birds.

Steller's jay

Yellow rumped warbler

Yellowstone National Park 59

Frogs, Snakes and More!

It's not just fur and feathers. These slippery and scaly creatures are important in Yellowstone's animal kingdom, too!

Tiger salamander

Four types of amphibians are common in Yellowstone: boreal chorus frogs, Columbia spotted frogs, western tiger salamanders, and western toads. A rarer species is the plains spadefoot toad. There is only one population in Yellowstone known to be actively breeding. Spadefoots can be hard to find: they spend most of their time underground.

Boreal chorus frog

Columbia spotted frog

Despite their name, common garter snakes are becoming *less* common in Yellowstone. Their relatives, terrestrial garter snakes, are the park's most common reptile.

Rubber boas tend to stay hidden and are most active at night, so it's unusual to see one. If you do, let a ranger know!

Prairie rattlesnakes are Yellowstone's only dangerously venomous snake. Bullsnakes look and act like rattlesnakes and are sometimes mistaken for them, but they are not dangerous.

The only non-snake reptile native to Yellowstone is the sagebrush lizard.

Arctic grayling

Native fish include Arctic grayling, mottled sculpin, mountain whitefish, westslope cutthroat trout, and Yellowstone cutthroat trout. Some non-native (invasive) fish species, like rainbow trout, have caused native species to become endangered. Park officials are working to stop them from taking over.

Yellowstone National Park

What People Do in Yellowstone

It takes a lot of people to keep Yellowstone going. About 750 people work in the park all year long, and twice that many during the busy summer season!

Park rangers in 1933.

Out in the park, rangers do things like patrol the lakes, remove litter from geysers, fight fires, maintain trails, and install bear boxes. The park even has its own search-and-rescue team.

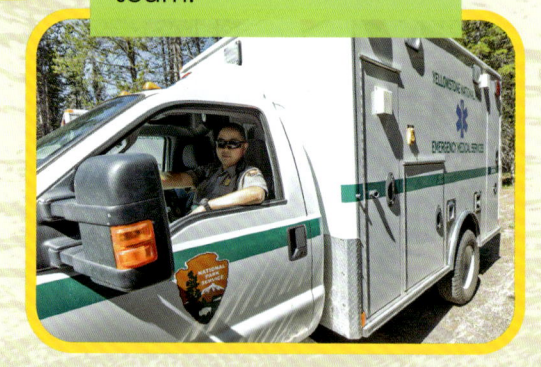

Park Rangers get you where you're going (and sometimes get you out of where you shouldn't be!) They also answer gazillions of questions and generally keep an eye on things.

Rangers run educational programs, create and maintain visitor exhibits, and predict geyser eruptions.

Scientists are always working in Yellowstone. You might find them managing bison herds, studying what grizzly bears eat, or photographing bugs. They also look for archaeological finds, measure stream flows, and take the temperature of hot springs.

Keeping visitors comfortable is a big job, too! Lots of people work at Yellowstone's lodges, restaurants, and stores. Most of these are summer jobs, and workers live in the park for the season.

Yellowstone National Park

Eating in Yellowstone

Vacation is hard work . . . good thing Yellowstone has lots of places to fuel up along the way! There is everything from full-service, sit-down meals to cafeterias, delis, and snack bars. Here are a few:

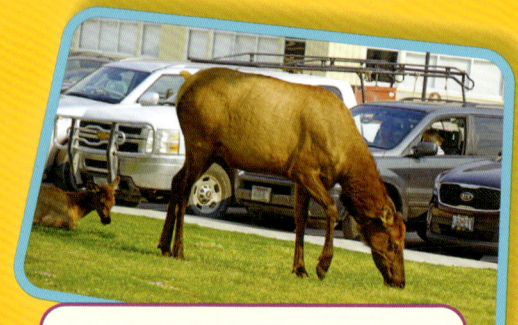

Watch elk graze out the window from the restaurant at **Mammoth Hotel Dining Room**, which serves special dishes from the region. It's more expensive, but the food is worth it.

Roosevelt Lodge offers Old West cookouts complete with a wagon ride. You'll need to make reservations well in advance, so plan ahead.

FAST FACT
Every day is better with ice cream! Don't miss the park's special huckleberry-flavored ice cream.

The **Canyon Soda Fountain** has an old-fashioned feel, and serves sandwiches, burgers, and some vegetarian choices.

If you're just outside the park, you can grab a burger at **The Corral** in nearby Gardiner, Montana. **The Wild West Pizzeria** in West Yellowstone, Montana, is another good bet.

No Lines!
Stock up at one of several general stores in the park, and pack a picnic to eat whenever you're ready. You'll find picnic areas with great views! Just remember:
* Never feed animals (including birds).
* Dispose of trash properly so that wildlife aren't tempted by it.
* Don't build campfires for cooking unless there's a fire grate (camp stoves and self-contained grills are okay).

Yellowstone National Park 65

Sweating in Yellowstone

Get off the road! That's the way to experience the best of Yellowstone.

Hiking is one of the most popular ways to see Yellowstone's hidden treasures. Dozens of different hikes take you past the park's big attractions, and many trails are close to parking lots for a quick way to stretch your legs. Some hikes are short and easy, like the Brink of the Lower Falls, which is less than a mile. Others are long and hard, like the 7-mile hike to the top of Mount Washburn. Check online or at ranger stations to see what's best for you.

Two-wheeling: Regular and electric bikes are another way to slow down and see the scenery. Bikes have to share the road with cars, though, so be careful. They're also not allowed on hiking trails or boardwalks.

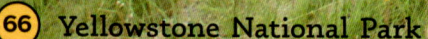

66 Yellowstone National Park

See it from the saddle: Take a guided tour on **horseback** with a private company. There are also horses you can rent for an hour or two.

Pack it In: Take a longer trip by using mules or llamas as pack animals for all your gear.

In the winter, try **snowshoeing** or **cross-country skiing** (see more winter fun on page 70).

Bear Spray

If you're in the backcountry, carry and practice using a can of bear spray. It creates a misty cloud that temporarily confuses bears so you can get away, but it won't hurt the animals.

BEAR SPRAY RENTALS

Yellowstone National Park 67

On the Water

Get a different view of Yellowstone from a boat. The lakes all have their own rules, but in general, kayaks and canoes are allowed. Motorboats are okay on Yellowstone and Lewis Lakes. Jet skis and water skis can't be used anywhere.

Go fishing! Get a permit and drop your line to see what bites. All native fish must be released back into the water, but you can keep (and cook) any non-native fish you catch.

68 Yellowstone National Park

Most of Yellowstone's lakes and rivers are far too cold for **swimming**, and it's not allowed throughout most of the park, but there are a couple of exceptions.
• The Firehole Swim area, located on the Firehole River, is open to swimmers beginning in mid-summer. (It's closed before that because of high water and strong currents.)
• Near Mammoth Hot Springs, cold water from the Gardner River mixes with hot water from the Boiling River hot spring (left). The result is just perfect for a warm soak!

Conditions in Yellowstone change all the time. Some areas might be closed, so be sure to check in advance!

Yellowstone National Park

Winter in Yellowstone

It's more challenging to see Yellowstone in the winter, but it's worth it. Most roads in the park close from November to April. Once the snow starts, the only way in is to take a snowmobile or snowcoach. You can sign up for a guided tour or get a permit to take your own snowmobile.

Yellowstone National Park

Rules of the road A few trails have set track for skiiers, but if it's not plowed, it's fair game for snowshoeing and cross-country skiing. There are lots of ski trails for all ability levels. Beginners can try the Old Canyon Bridge Ski Trail for a short ski that takes you along the Yellowstone River. There's also the Indian Creek Loop, for some great views of the Mammoth area.

Digging Out Yellowstone can get up to 15 to 20 feet of snow in the winter. Using a fleet of bulldozers and snowplows, it takes about a month for park crews to clear all the roads!

Safety Tips:
• Never ski alone
• Stay on trails, especially near geothermal areas
• Dress in layers and drink plenty of water
• Check with a park ranger in advance to get an update on the latest conditions

Warm Up! Several "warming huts" are located throughout the park. Many have food and water available, and some are open 24 hours.

Yellowstone National Park

Winter in Yellowstone

Animals are used to Yellowstone's harsh weather. They have lots of ways to adapt!

Many animals move to the park's lower elevations, where it's warmer. You'll also see bison, elk, and other animals gathering beside the park's natural heaters—geysers and hot springs.

Mammals grow thicker fur in the winter, with an undercoat and an overcoat. Some have hollow hairs with air inside, which provides insulation. They can even control how their fur moves, so they can fluff it up to trap warm air.

Bears just go to sleep for the season. They build up fat in summer, then hole up in dens around November and hibernate until spring. They don't eat, drink, or go to the bathroom for five months!

It's tough to travel through several feet of snow. Moose have joints that allow them to swing their legs over the top of the snow, instead of having to plow through it. Bison have thick, strong necks that swing their big heads to clear snow that's up to three feet high.

Chorus frogs actually form ice in their veins! Their hearts stop and they don't breathe. They can stay that way for several months. But when the weather warms up in early spring, they thaw and everything goes back to normal.

Smaller animals like rodents and grouse burrow underground for protection from the cold.

Yellowstone National Park

Places to Stay

Are you a fancy hotel type? Or do you like a cozy cabin? Whatever you like, Yellowstone has lots to choose from. (If you're a camper, turn the page.)

Old Faithful Inn: Electric lights! Steam heat! When the Old Faithful Inn first opened in 1904, these things were a big deal for Yellowstone guests. The inn is built from the logs of lodgepole pines that grew in the park, and has a massive stone fireplace. Observation decks offer great views of Old Faithful and other geysers.

Lake Yellowstone Hotel and Cottages: A central hotel and lots of surrounding cottages are perfect if you want to spend time on the lake.

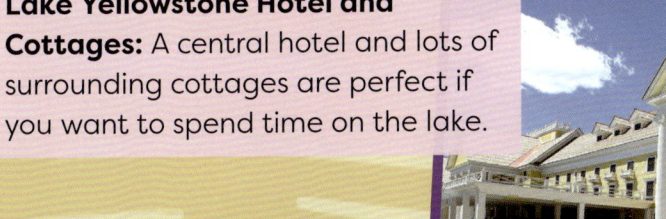

Although most Yellowstone accommodations are only open in summer, **Mammoth Hot Springs Hotel and Cabins** are open year-round. Check out the map room in the main hotel: this map of the United States is made from 15 different kinds of wood.

Roosevelt Lodge and Cabins This was named for President Theodore Roosevelt, but there's no evidence he actually camped here. The lodge and cabins in northern Yellowstone weren't built until after he visited in 1903.

Canyon Lodge and Cabins is Yellowstone's largest place to stay. It has more than 500 rooms and cabins!

Yellowstone National Park 75

PLACES TO CAMP

Sleeping under the stars is fun anywhere, but the great outdoors is *really* great here! There are more than 2,000 sites at the park's 12 campgrounds, but many are first-come, first-served, and they fill up fast, so get there early. Here are some of the most popular:

FAST FACT
How to pack: It's easy to forget the bug spray, or the can opener, or the toilet paper. Check online for lists of stuff you'll definitely want to have with you.

Enjoy great views of Yellowstone Lake and the surrounding mountains from **Bridge Bay Campground**.

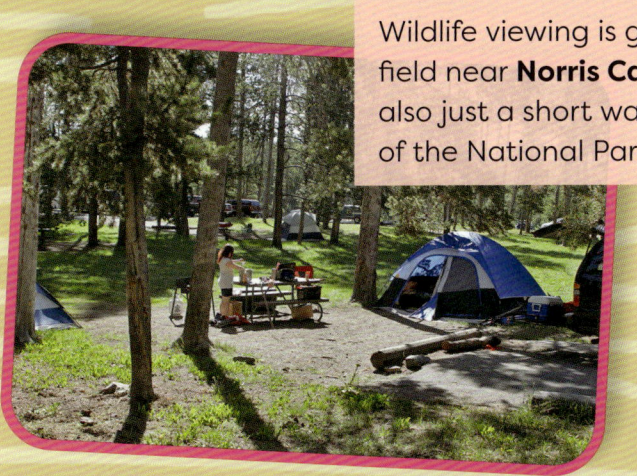

Wildlife viewing is good in the open field near **Norris Campground**. It's also just a short walk to the Museum of the National Park Ranger.

The **Grant Village Campground** goes beyond the basics, with a general store and a restaurant and gas station nearby.

Elk and bison sometimes wander through the **Mammoth Hot Springs Campground**, the only campground open year-round. It's near lots of good fishing and hiking, too.

Keep it under wraps!

Bears love food, especially *your* food. Even if you can't smell it, they can. Keep your food in a locked car or one of the park's many bear-proof boxes. Don't leave trash, either. It's not only ugly; it's bear bait!

Yellowstone National Park 77

CAMPFIRE SONGS AND TRADITIONS

Even if you're not camping, you can still enjoy an evening by the campfire (and you don't even have to collect the wood)! Many of the lodges offer outdoor presentations about parts of the park (check bulletin boards in the park for details).

It's always fun to sing campfire classics like "Home on the Range" and "This Land Is Your Land" when you're settling in for the night. But did you know that Yellowstone lodges all used to have songs that were about their particular areas? Here's one from—well, you can probably guess. It's sung to the tune of "My Darling Clementine":

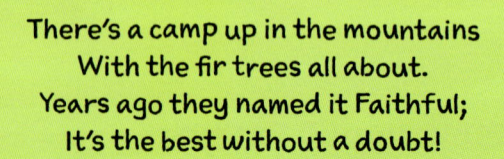

There's a camp up in the mountains
With the fir trees all about.
Years ago they named it Faithful;
It's the best without a doubt!

You will find the camps inviting
as you journey through the Park,
But there's none can beat Old Faithful,
if you're out just for a lark.

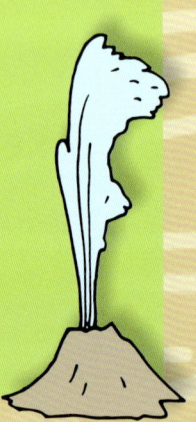

Yellowstone National Park

S'mores:

The best dessert ever is also one of the easiest. Whip these up over your campfire:

* Break a graham cracker into two squares.
* Put pieces of a chocolate bar on one half and set aside.
* Toast a marshmallow over the fire.
* Place it on top of the chocolate.
* Make a sandwich with the other graham cracker square.
* Squish (gently!) and eat.

Yellowstone National Park

LOL!
Yellowstone Jokes

The bison and bears won't get these jokes, but we hope you will! Here are some jokes and riddles to tickle your funny bone.

What's a Yellowstone guide's favorite TV show?

Ranger Things

When are Yellowstone campers very, very serious?

When they're being *intense*! (In tents, get it?)

How do Yellowstone mountains stay warm?

They put on their snowcaps!

What's the name of Yellowstone's overpowered drinking fountain?

Old Face-full

How can you tell Old Faithful is angry?

It's always blowing off steam!

How do grizzlies catch salmon in the Yellowstone River?

With their bear hands!

Why are some Yellowstone hikes easy?

They're a walk in the Park!

How do father buffaloes say farewell to their boys?

Bison!

Yellowstone National Park

Spooky Sights

There's so much to do in Yellowstone that lots of people just want to stay forever—and some do! If you get a chill when you're at these places, it might not be from the weather.

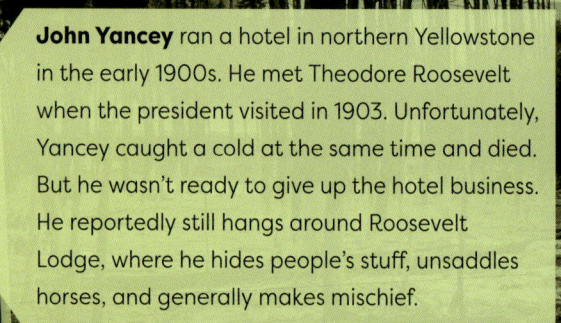

John Yancey ran a hotel in northern Yellowstone in the early 1900s. He met Theodore Roosevelt when the president visited in 1903. Unfortunately, Yancey caught a cold at the same time and died. But he wasn't ready to give up the hotel business. He reportedly still hangs around Roosevelt Lodge, where he hides people's stuff, unsaddles horses, and generally makes mischief.

In 1886, **Mattie Culver** moved into the Firehole area, where her new husband worked. She loved Yellowstone, but died only a few years later from tuberculosis. She was buried near their home, and some people say they still see her spirit walking along the river.

82 Yellowstone National Park

Need help with your bags? If you're staying at the **Lake Yellowstone Hotel**, look for a friendly bellman, dressed in early 1900s clothes, who will carry stuff upstairs for you. He knows the place pretty well—he's worked here for more than 100 years, even if some of them have been as a ghost!

In 1915, a newlywed couple got in a fight at the **Old Faithful Inn**. The bride was then found dead with her head cut off. Her ghostly figure later appeared—and she was carrying her own head! Are you creeped out? Don't be—a former manager of the hotel admitted he made up the whole story in the 1990s.

Yellowstone National Park 83

YELLOWSTONE BY THE NUMBERS

Stats and facts and digits galore! Here are some of the numbers that make Yellowstone what it is.

11,358 FEET
Yellowstone's highest point, at Eagle Peak

1,000
Miles of hiking trails

1,800
Archaeological sites in the park

672 miles
Length of the Yellowstone River

84 Yellowstone National Park

30–35 million pounds of plants that Yellowstone's grazing animals eat each year.

1,500–2,000 Annual earthquakes (most are too small for people to feel)

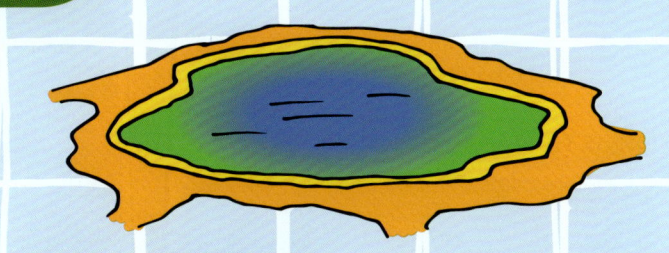

10,000 hydrothermal features (about 500 are geysers)

4.2 million-plus Record number of visitors in a year (2016)

Yellowstone National Park

Not Far Away

As if Yellowstone was not enough, other nearby sites offer other ways to explore the natural beauty and history of the area.

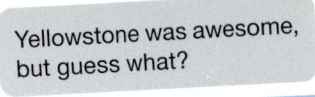

Yellowstone was awesome, but guess what?

A bear ate your phone?

LOL! No, we went to another national park just to the south of Yellowstone.

South Yellowstone National Park?

👎 Grand Teton National Park!

Pretty beautiful!

Grand Teton started in 1929, but they added more land over the years.

You mean they built more mountains!

Ha! No, the Park Service included more area. By 1950, the park was the size it is today—485 square miles!

That's much smaller than Yellowstone.

But much taller. The tallest peaks tower almost 14,000 feet!

Yellowstone National Park

Grand Teton is a great place to hike and bike.

As opposed to shake and bake.

Uh . . . yes. I guess. Annnnyway, we rented bikes to use on a long bike trail.

Ride on!

And on this hiking trip, we saw a moose munching in the water! 😁

The park has lots of lakes to explore, too.

I like lakes!

Jenny Lake was perfect for canoeing.

And after we finished, we camped nearby.

Hope you had "s-more" fun there!

Yum! Yes!

Yellowstone National Park

Not Far Away

Later, we headed west. Just beyond the Yellowstone entrance there was a really cool museum.

What did you see?

We climbed on a stagecoach, checked out old-time tour buses, and read about earthquakes and fires in Yellowstone.

Hope you didn't feel any!

Nope, steady as a rock at the Museum of the Yellowstone! We also saw a huge stuffed grizzly.

How did you "bear it?" LOL

Ugh! Actually, it was cool . . . and enormous. Its name was Snaggletooth!

Yellowstone National Park

Outside the east side of the park we found a STACK of museums!

> A museum about stacks? Not very interesting.

No, the **Buffalo Bill Center** has FIVE museums to explore.

One was the **Whitney Western Art Museum**. Awesome paintings and sculpture.

Another was all about the famous Buffalo Bill Cody himself.

At the **Plains Indians Museum**, we saw more beautiful artwork.

There was also an exhibit on how people used to live in the area hundreds of years ago.

And we even saw toys that Plains kids used back then.

> Sounds like a cool day. Come home soon—I miss you!

Yellowstone National Park **89**

Other Amazing Parks

The movement that started Yellowstone in 1872 has kept going. As of 2022, the United States was home to 63 national parks. And there are more than 4,000 around the world. The idea of preserving nature and its beauty for the future is one that just keeps growing! Here's a short look at some other well-known and popular U.S. national parks.

Yosemite National Park: This park was the third national park, but it was the first place that the federal government protected land. President Abraham Lincoln signed a law in 1864 protecting parts of what became Yosemite, which is in California. The park is famous for the Half Dome rock and "fire" waterfalls. Yosemite Falls is one of the tallest in the country.

Grand Canyon National Park: Home to one of the most famous places on the planet, this park features a mile-deep canyon formed by the Colorado River. The canyon is as big as the entire state of Rhode Island! People visit the North and South Rims of the canyon to take in the incredible views. More adventurous folks take mule rides or hike to the bottom of the canyon.

Great Smoky Mountains: This Tennessee park is the most popular, with more than 12 million visitors each year. It is named for the mountain range in Tennessee and North Carolina that makes up most of the park. It gets so many visitors partly because it's so large. They come from all over to hike, backpack, bicycle, and more.

Zion National Park: Carved by the Virgin River in southern Utah, Zion was once home to the ancient Anasazi people. Remains of their cliff dwellings are just one of the many sights in this beautiful, mountainous park. Hikers love exploring the many canyons made by the river.

Channel Islands: National parks are not just on the mainland. Seven are all or partially on islands. One is easy to reach. Five small islands make up this park off the coast of California, a short boat ride from millions of coastal residents. Santa Cruz is the largest and hikers, campers, and kayakers love exploring its trails and campsites.

Yellowstone National Park

FIND OUT MORE!
Websites, Books, and More!

Web Sites

National Park Service, Yellowstone
https://www.nps.gov/yell

Yellowstone National Park Trips
https://www.yellowstonepark.com

United States Geological Survey
https://www.usgs.gov/volcanoes/yellowstone

Museum of the Yellowstone:
https://www.museumoftheyellowstone.org

Grizzly and Wolf Discovery Center:
https://www.grizzlyctr.givecloud.co

Whitney Western Art Museum:
https://www.centerofthewest.org/our-museums/western-art/

Yellowstone Art Museum:
https://www.artmuseum.org

Books

Barr, Catherine. *Fourteen Wolves: A Rewilding Story.* New York: Bloomsbury Children's Books, 2022.

The National Parks: Lands of Wonder. New York: DK Publishing, 2020.

Silber, Kate, and Clare Grace. *National Parks of the USA: Activity Book.* New York: Wide-Eyed Editions, 2020.

Koontz, Robin. *Natural Laboratories: Scientists in National Parks: Yellowstone.* Vero Beach, FL: Rourke Educational Media, 2019.

Noel, Karl. *Yellowstone National Park.* Minneapolis: Gray Duck Creative Works, 2018.

Photo Credits and Thanks

Photos from Dreamstime, Library of Congress, National Archives, Shutterstock, or Wikimedia. Photos are also from the National Park Service media center as well as its extensive historical collection. Jim Peaco/NPS took the wolf release photos on page 54-55. Thanks to Old Town Trail for 24L.

Artwork by Lemonade Pixel. Maps on page 6-7 by Jessica Nevins.

Thanks to our pals Nancy Ellwood, Kait Leggett, and the fine folks at Arcadia!

INDEX

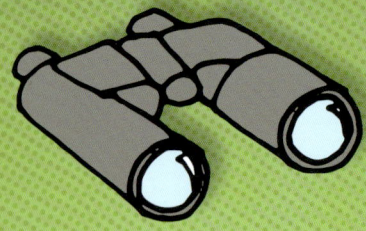

Adams, Ansel 44-45
Albright Visitor Center 46
Arapaho people 27

Baggley Herma 49
Blacktail Plateau Drive 40
Bridge Bay Campground 76
Bridger, Jim 18
Brown, Grafton Tyler 42
Buffalo Bill Center 89

Canary Spring 37
Canyon Lodge 75
Canyon Soda Fountain 65
Canyon Visitor Education Center 47
Channel Islands National Park 91
Colter, John 9, 18, 24
Crow people 10, 16
Culver, Mattie 82

Davis, Sarah 48
Dragon's Mouth Spring 26

East Entrance Road 40, 41

Firehole Swim Area 69
First Peoples Mountain 27
Fishing Bridge Visitor Center 59
Flathead people 10, 16
Fossil Forest 36

Gardner River 69
Grand Canyon National Park 90
Grand Canyon of the Yellowstone 38
Grand Geyser 33
Grand Loop 40
Grand Prismatic Spring 12-13
Grand Teton National Park 6, 86-87
Grant, President Ulysses 9
Grant Village Campground 77
Great Smoky Mountains National Park 91

Hayden Expedition 9, 19
Hayden, Ferdinand 19, 24
Hayden Valley 39
Haynes, Frank 43
Hidatsa people 10, 11

Indian Creek Loop 71
Island Park Caldera 14

Jackson, William Henry 19, 43

Kepler Cascades 35
Kiowa people 26

Lake Yellowstone Hotel and Cottages 75, 83
Lamar Valley 39, 40
Lewis & Clark Expedition 9, 24
Lindsley, Marguerite 48

Mammoth Hotel 64, 75
Mammoth Hot Springs 37, 40, 69
Mammoth Hot Springs Campground 77
McCartney Hotel, 20

94 Yellowstone National Park

Moran, Thomas 19, 43
Morning Glory Pool 32
mudpots 33
Museum of the National Park Ranger 46
Museum of the Yellowstone 88

National Bison Legacy Act 53
National Park Rangers 46, 48, 49, 62, 63,
National Park Service 22, 45, 46
Norris Geyser Basin Museum 40, 47
Norris Campground 77
Norris, Philetus 25

Obsidian Cliffs 16, 36
Old Canyon Bridge Ski Trail 71
Old Faithful 31, 81
Old Faithful Inn 21, 74, 83

Plains Indians Museums 89

Riverside Geyser 33
Roosevelt Corral 36
Roosevelt Lodge and Cabins 64, 75
Roosevelt, President Theodore 21

Shoshone Lake 27
s'mores 79
Steamboat Geyser 32

TEDDY 41
Tower Fall 35
Tukudika people 17

Wahhi Falls 27
Whitney Western Art Museum 42, 89
Wind River Reservation 27

Yellowstone Art Museum
Yellowstone Art & Photography Center
Yellowstone Caldera 15
Yellowstone Falls 35
Yellowstone Lake 16, 34, 68
Yellowstone River 6, 11, 34, 71, 81
Yancey, John 82
Yount, Harry 25
Younts Peak 6
Yosemite National Park 90

Zion National Park 91

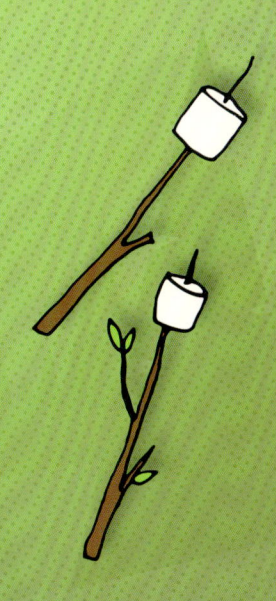

Thanks for Visiting

Yellowstone National Park

Come Back Soon!